The Magic of Love

Love is a treasure full of surprise!
Can you discover where it might hide?

written by
Stephanie Franco

illustrated by
Amy Wilkening

Photo Credit for Bio Photos:
Author photograph by Tony Franco
Illustrator photograph by Michelle Cervantez

Balboa Press books may be ordered through booksellers or by contacting:

Balboa Press
A Division of Hay House
1663 Liberty Drive
Bloomington, IN 47403
www.balboapress.com
1 (877) 407-4847

ISBN: 978-1-5043-2732-9 (sc)
ISBN: 978-1-5043-2733-6 (e)

Library of Congress Control Number: 2015901438

Print information available on the last page.

Balboa Press rev. date: 10/16/2015

BALBOA
PRESS
A DIVISION OF HAY HOUSE

For all beings, young and old, who believe in the power of love. ~S.F. & A.W.

Thank you Kathie Kommor, my dear mamma,
for helping make my dreams come true.

~ S.F.

The MAGIC of LOVE plays
hide and go seek, so come play
along and let's take a peek!

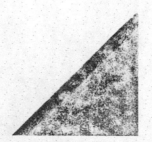

Love is a treasure full of surprise! Can
you discover where it might hide?

Love is everywhere and it's felt all around.
It circles our world like a merry-go-round.

Love is the light that shines from
the sun, sending golden rays to
everything and everyone.

Love blows the wind that swirls
through the trees. Love paints the
colors on the bright autumn leaves.

Love moves the tides in and out
with grace. Love is the surprise
of the moon's changing face.

Love is the raindrops that fill a
big, puffy cloud. It's the sound of
thunder bursting out loud.

Love grows the garden that makes
your food taste so yummy. Love is
the feeling of a thankful tummy.

Love is the *smack* of a fish's lips kiss. It
opens sweet flowers blooming with bliss.

Love is the root of a tree, tall and
proud. Love spreads support and
encouragement all around.

Love is the warmth of your mother's
embrace when tears of sadness are
streaming slowly down your face.

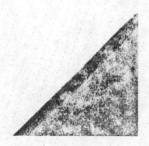

24

Love is the wiggle in your cute little walk
and the musical tune sung in your talk.

Love is the twinkle in your favorite star.
Love is the joy of being who you are!

Love is the *roar* of the lion's gruff
voice. Love is how you feel when
you make a good choice.

Love makes the sound of your heart's
rhythmic beat. Can you hear it?
Thump. Thump. You are unique!

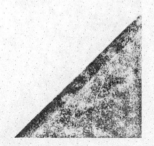

Love is the feeling you feel inside when you
listen to your heart and take its wise advice.

Love has watched over you from the
time of your birth. Love is trusting
yourself and feeling self-worth.

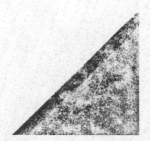

Love soars through the air on an
eagle's winged flight. Love graces
the world with peace and delight.

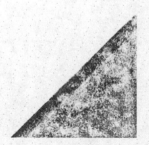

Love is the hope that together we can all live peacefully. Love connects our mind, body, heart, and spirit to a great mystery.

Love is a place of inner peace and wonder,
a glorious place in which we can ponder.

Hug yourself. Draw into your core. Do you feel your tiny self becoming more and more?

Shine out with that love from limb
to limb, moving out into the world
but always coming from within!

Now, take a deep breath and honor your place of stillness and truth. Smile! How does it feel to know LOVE is YOU?

Meet the Author
Stephanie Franco, MA, Ed.

One of Stephanie's dreams has always been to publish books for children and adults that inspire, empower, and serve to make the world a more peaceful, loving place. Her heart couldn't be happier to share this message of boundless love! A Masters in Elementary Education led her to teach students from diverse cultures for over a decade. She continues to follow her heart and uplift others by serving as a Reiki Practitioner, Mindfulness Trainer, and a Contributing Author for LightworkersWorld.com. Stephanie and her amazing husband, Tony, find great happiness living in the *now,* traveling the world, and exploring the delightful Rocky Mountains surrounding their Denver, Colorado home. Visit stephaniefranco.com to discover more.

Meet the Illustrator
Amy Wilkening

Amy began to creatively express herself at a very young age. She started her career studying Graphic Design and soon after started her own business painting murals for both kids and adults. Art, drawing, crafts and design have always been an important part of her life, but using her artistic gifts to benefit children in any way is her passion. Illustrating children's books has been a dream of hers that has finally come true! Amy has lived most of her life in Littleton, Colorado. She is the Co-Founder of FaithandAngelsMovement.com.

Meet the Creative Collaborators

Kathie Kommor, MA, LPC

As a Licensed Professional Counselor, parent and parenting educator, Kathie has always been committed to supporting and encouraging the development of our self worth as a foundation of our movement through life. Kathie lives in Charleston, West Virginia and is the mother of Stephanie Franco.

Michelle Cervantez, MA, Ed.

Michelle's passion resides in teaching, writing, healing and learning. Her life purpose has been devoted to children for over 20 years. She taught in public schools with a Masters in Elementary Education and Endorsement in English Language Acquisition. Michelle changed careers to become a writer and founded FaithandAngelsMovement.com.

nted in the United States
Bookmasters